THE LITTLE BOOK OF
SHAKESPEARE

Published in 2022 by OH!
An Imprint of Welbeck Non-Fiction Limited,
part of Welbeck Publishing Group.
Based in London and Sydney.
www.welbeckpublishing.com

Compilation text © Welbeck Non-Fiction Limited 2022
Design © Welbeck Non-Fiction Limited 2022

ISBN 978-1-80069-192-6

Written and compiled by: Stella Caldwell
Project manager: Russell Porter
Design: Andy Jones
Production: Jess Brisley

A CIP catalogue record for this book is available from the British Library

Printed in China

10 9 8 7 6 5 4 3 2 1

THE LITTLE BOOK OF
SHAKESPEARE

THE BEST OF THE BARD

CONTENTS

INTRODUCTION

"He was not of an age, but for all time!" wrote Shakespeare's contemporary and literary rival Ben Jonson in his elegy "To the Memory of My Beloved the Author, Mr William Shakespeare". Some may argue that Jonson's praise was not altogether sincere, but 450 years after the Bard's birth, he is widely celebrated as the world's greatest and most influential writer.

There can be little doubt that Shakespeare had an astonishing command of the English language. Indeed, he demonstrated a greater range of expression than perhaps any writer in any language. Renowned scholar Louis Marder wrote, "Shakespeare was so facile in employing words that he was able to use over 7,000 of them – more than occur in the whole King James version of the Bible – only once and never again." *The Oxford English Dictionary* credits Shakespeare with coining around 1,600 words. But not only did the writer invent totally new words but he also experimented with existing language with wit, flair and imagination.

Aside from his astonishing talent for words, Shakespeare's genius lay in his sheer dramatic skill and ability to create richly imagined characters. He was a masterful observer of the human condition: love, hate, joy, jealousy, pride, fear, vanity – Shakespeare looked deep inside the human soul and saw that human nature is unpredictable and can never be defined in simple terms. That is why his works retain so much relevance for audiences today.

The Little Book of Shakespeare contains more than 150 of the writer's best-loved quotes, as well as fascinating facts about his life and achievements. Containing startling insights, witty asides and wise advice, and covering universal themes from love and friendship to courage, treachery and ambition, these timeless quotes showcase some of the finest lines ever crafted in the English language.

CHAPTER

one

The Course of True Love

The word "love" appears more than 2,000 times in Shakespeare's works — and that's not counting words like "beloved" or "loving". The following selection of quotes are proof that the Bard had plenty to say about matters of the heart.

What is love? 'tis not hereafter,
Present mirth hath present laughter;
What's to come is still unsure.
In delay there lies no plenty;
Then come kiss me, sweet and twenty:
Youth's a stuff will not endure.

Twelfth Night, Act 2, Scene 3

"

Love is not love
Which alters when it alteration finds,
Or bends with the remover
to remove.
O no! it is an ever-fixed mark
That looks on tempests and is
never shaken.

"

Sonnet 116

"

Who ever loved that loved not at first sight?

"

As You Like It, Act 3, Scene 5

Love comforeth like sunshine after rain,
But Lust's effect is tempest after sun;
Love's gentle spring doth always fresh remain;
Lust's winter comes ere summer half be done;
Love surfeits not, Lust like a glutton dies;
Love is all truth, Lust full of forged lies.

Venus and Adonis

"

But love is blind, and
lovers cannot see
The pretty follies that
themselves commit...

"

The Merchant of Venice, Act 2, Scene 6

"

Why, there's a wench! Come on, and kiss me, Kate.

"

The Taming of the Shrew, Act 5, Scene 1

But thy eternal summer shall not fade
Nor lose possession of that fair thou owest,
Nor shall death brag thou wander'st in his shade,
When in eternal lines to time thou grow'st:
So long as men can breathe, or eyes can see,
So long lives this, and this gives life to thee.

Sonnet 18

"

My bounty is as boundless
as the sea,

My love as deep. The more
I give to thee,

The more I have, for both are
infinite.

"

Romeo and Juliet, Act 2, Scene 2

" There's beggary in the love that can be reckoned. "

Antony and Cleopatra, Act 1, Scene 1

Nobody can be sure of William Shakespeare's precise date of birth, although records show that he was baptized in Stratford-upon-Avon, England, on 26 April 1564.

It was the custom in Elizabethan times for children to be baptized when they were three days old, so we can assume his birthday was on 23 April.

What's in a name? That
which we call a rose
By any other word would
smell as sweet.

Romeo and Juliet, Act 2, Scene 2

"

I pray you do not fall in
love with me,
For I am falser than vows
made in wine.

"

As You Like It, **Act 3, Scene 5**

"

Sigh no more, ladies,
sigh no more,
Men were deceivers ever,
One foot in sea
and one on shore,
To one thing constant never.

Much Ado About Nothing, Act 2, Scene 3

"
O, swear not by the moon,
th' inconstant moon,
That monthly changes in her
circle orb,
Lest that thy love prove
likewise variable.
"

Romeo and Juliet, Act 2, Scene 2

A lover's eyes will gaze an eagle blind.
A lover's ear will hear the lowest sound
When the suspicious head of theft is stopped.
Love's feeling is more soft and sensible
Than are the tender horns of cockled snails...
... And when Love speaks, the voice of
all the gods
Make heaven drowsy with the harmony.

Love's Labour's Lost, Act 4, Scene 3

ROSALIND:
Now tell me how long you would have her after you have possessed her.

ORLANDO:
For ever and a day.

As You Like It, Act 4, Scene 1

"

Love is a smoke raised with
the fume of sighs;
Being purged, a fire sparkling in
lovers' eyes;
Being vexed, a sea nourished with
loving tears.
What is it else? A madness most discreet,

A choking gall and a preserving sweet.

"

Romeo and Juliet, Act 1, Scene 1

If music be the food of love,
play on.
Give me excess of it, that,
surfeiting,
The appetite may sicken and
so die.

Twelfth Night, Act 1, Scene 1

The barge she sat in, like a burnished throne,
Burned on the water.
The poop was beaten gold,
Purple the sails, and so perfumèd that
The winds were lovesick with them.
The oars were silver,
Which to the tune of flutes kept stroke,
and made
The water which they beat to follow faster,
As amorous of their strokes.

Antony and Cleopatra, Act 2, Scene 2

Shakespeare's father, John, was a glove-maker, and his mother, Mary, was the daughter of a local farmer. John became a successful businessman, although his illegal dealings as a wool trader – he was not licensed to be one – landed him in trouble with the law.

William was the third of eight children, three of whom died in infancy or childhood.

"

The course of true love never did run smooth...

"

A *Midsummer Night's Dream*, Act 1, Scene 1

"

hear my soul speak:
The very instant that
I saw you, did
My heart fly to your
service...

"

The Tempest, Act 3, Scene 1

"

Good night, good night!
Parting is such
sweet sorrow,
That I shall say good
night till it be morrow.

Romeo and Juliet, Act 2, Scene 2

"

So are you to my
thoughts as food to life,
Or as sweet-seasoned
showers are to
the ground.

"

Sonnet 75

"

Thy sweet love remembered
such wealth brings
That then I scorn to change
my state with kings.

"

Sonnet 29

"

Love looks not with the
eyes, but with the mind,
And therefore is winged
Cupid painted blind.

""

A Midsummer Night's Dream, Act 1, Scene 1

"

O, wither'd is the garland
of the war,
The soldier's pole is fall'n:
young boys and girls
Are level now with men;
the odds is gone,
And there is nothing
left remarkable
Beneath the visiting moon.

Antony and Cleopatra, Act 4, Scene 15

It is likely that Shakespeare was educated at King Edward VI School in Stratford-upon-Avon, which is still standing today.

He probably started his education at the age of seven or so and left at 14. Lessons would have included the study of Latin and possibly classical Greek, as well as the works of classical authors and dramatists, such as Ovid, Horace and Virgil.

"

When you depart from me, sorrow abides and happiness takes his leave.

"

Much Ado About Nothing, Act 1, Scene 1

At the age of 18, Shakespeare married 26-year-old Anne Hathaway. She was already several months pregnant and hasty arrangements must have been made for their wedding – a child born out of wedlock would have been scandalous.

The married couple lived with Shakespeare's parents in Stratford-Upon-Avon, where their first child, Susanna, was born in 1583. Their twins, Judith and Hamnet, followed in 1585.

CHAPTER

two

Why, Courage Then!

Shakespeare returned to the theme of
honour and courage — or the lack of these
virtues — time and time again in his plays.
Indeed, he saw these qualities as the defining
characteristics of a good person. Here are some
of his finest words on the subject.

Cowards die many times
before their deaths;
The valiant never taste of
death but once.

Julius Caesar, **Act 2, Scene 2**

"

I, that with my sword
Quartered the world, and o'er green
Neptune's back
With ships made cities, condemn myself to lack
The courage of a woman; less noble mind
Than she which by her death our Caesar tells
'I am conqueror of myself.'

"

Antony and Cleopatra, Act 4, Scene 14

That's a valiant flea that dare eat his breakfast on the lip of a lion.

Henry V, Act 3, Scene 7

Art thou afeard
To be the same in thine
own act and valour
As thou are in desire?

Macbeth, Act 1, Scene 7

He excels his brother for a
coward; yet his brother is
reputed one of the best that is.
In a retreat he outruns
any lackey: marry, in coming on
he has the cramp.

All's Well That Ends Well, Act 4, Scene 3

Following the birth of Shakespeare's twins, in 1585, there is no record of him again until 1592, when he emerges in London as an actor.

This seven-year period is often referred to as "the lost years".

There has been much speculation as to what Shakespeare was doing during this time. Some suggest that he served as a soldier or perhaps joined a travelling theatre troupe, but the truth is that he left no real clues.

Men at some time are masters
of their fates;
The fault, dear Brutus,
is not in our stars,
But in ourselves,
that we are underlings.

Julius Caesar, Act I, Scene 2

Who could refrain,
That had a heart to love,
and in that heart
Courage to make's love known?

Macbeth, Act 2, Scene 3

"

Conscience doth make cowards of us all.

"

Hamlet, Act 3, Scene 1

"

I told you, sir, they were red-hot
with drinking,
So full of valour that they
smote the air
For breathing in their faces,
beat the ground
For kissing of their feet...

"

The Tempest, Act 4, Scene 1

"

And thou a natural coward, without instinct.

"

Henry IV, Part 1, Act 2, Scene 4

In 1592, the playwright Robert Greene published *Greenes Groats-Worth of Witte*. The book contained criticism of his rivals, including this about Shakespeare:

"There is an upstart Crow, beautified with our feathers, that with his Tygers hart wrapt in a Players hyde, supposes he is as well able to bombast out a blanke verse as the best of you: and beeing an absolute Johannes fac totum, is in his owne conceit the onely Shake-scene in a countrey.

"

A thousand hearts are great
within my bosom:
Advance our standards, set upon our foes;
Our ancient word of courage,
fair Saint George,
Inspire us with the spleen of fiery dragons!
Upon them! Victory sits on our helms.

Richard III, Act 5, Scene 6

> **"**
> What's brave, what's noble,
> Let's do it after the high
> Roman fashion,
> And make death proud
> to take us.
> **"**

Antony and Cleopatra, Act 4, Scene 15

Be brave, then; for
your captain is brave,
and vows
reformation.

Henry VI, Part 2, Act 4, Scene 2

"

There's no better sign of a brave mind than a hard hand.

"

Henry VI, Part 2, Act 4, Scene 2

"

In a false quarrel there is no true valour.

"

Much Ado About Nothing, Act 5, Scene 1

Little is known about the relationship between Shakespeare and his wife, Anne, although we do know that his work in London meant they spent long periods apart. In Shakespeare's last will and testament, Anne was only mentioned once:

"Item I gyve unto my wife my second-best bed with the furniture."

"

Boldness be my friend: Arm me audacity from head to foot!

"

Cymbeline, Act 1, Scene 6

From around 1594, Shakespeare was part of a theatre company called "The Lord Chamberlain's Men". After the accession of James 1, in 1603, it became known as "The King's Men".

Boasting the famous actor Richard Burbage, the best theatre, the Globe, and the finest dramatist in Shakespeare, it's little wonder the company was highly successful.

O Romeo, Romeo, brave
Mercutio's dead!
That gallant spirit hath aspired
the clouds,
which too untimely here did
scorn the earth.

Romeo and Juliet, Act 3, Scene 1

"

The better part of valour is discretion...

"

Henry IV, Part 1, Act 5, Scene 4

CHAPTER

three

Is This a Dagger?

From "Macbeth" or "Hamlet" to "Julius Caesar" and "Antony and Cleopatra", the themes of ambition, loyalty, treachery and revenge — and the consequences of such human behaviour — are widely explored in Shakespeare's works.

"

Go forward, and be choked with thy ambition!

"

Henry VI, Part 1, Act 2, Scene 4

"

Uneasy lies the head that wears a crown.

"

King Henry IV, Part 2, Act 3, Scene 1

"

Let Rome in Tiber melt,
and the wide arch
Of the ranged empire fall.
Here is my space.
Kingdoms are clay.
Our dungy earth alike
Feeds beast as man.

"

Antony and Cleopatra, Act 1, Scene 1

"

My words fly up, my
thoughts remain below:
Words without thoughts
never to heaven go.

"

Hamlet, Act 3, Scene 3

"

Why, man, he doth bestride
the narrow world
Like a Colossus, and we petty men
Walk under his huge legs,
and peep about
To find ourselves
dishonourable graves.

Julius Caesar, Act 1, Scene 2

Shakespeare in Numbers

37 plays

10 tragedies

10 histories

17 comedies

154 sonnets

884,647 words

"

Is this a dagger which I see
before me,
The handle toward my hand?
Come, let me clutch thee:
I have thee not, and yet
I see thee still.

Macbeth, **Act 2, Scene 1**

Now is the winter of our discontent
Made glorious summer by this sun of York;
And all the clouds that lour'd upon our house
In the deep bosom of the ocean buried.
Now are our brows bound with victorious wreaths;
Our bruised arms hung up for monuments;
Our stern alarums changed to merry meetings,
Our dreadful marches to delightful measures.

Richard III, Act 1, Scene 1

This story shall the good man teach his son,
And Crispin Crispian shall ne'er go by,
From this day to the ending of the world,
But we in it shall be remembered;
We few, we happy few, we band of brothers.
For he to-day that sheds his blood with me
Shall be my brother.

Henry V, Act 4 Scene 3

If you prick us, do we not bleed? If you tickle us, do we not laugh? If you poison us, do we not die? And if you wrong us, shall we not revenge?

The Merchant of Venice, Act 3, Scene 1

Vengeance is in my heart,
death in my hand,
Blood and revenge are
hammering in my head.

***Titus Andronicus*, Act 2, Scene 3**

Aside from writing his plays and sonnets, Shakespeare was also a respected actor.

He performed in many of his own plays, and there is evidence that he took the roles of King Duncan in *Macbeth*, the ghost in *Hamlet* and Adam in *As You Like It*.

"

As, I confess, it is my
nature's plague
To spy into abuses,
and oft my jealousy
Shapes faults that are not...

"

Othello, Act 3, Scene 3

Friends, Romans, countrymen,
lend me your ears.
I come to bury Caesar,
not to praise him.
The evil that men do lives after them;
The good is oft interred with
their bones.
So let it be with Caesar.

Julius Caesar, Act 3, Scene 2

"

Et tu, Brute?

"

Julius Caesar, Act 3, Scene 1

"As Caesar loved me, I weep for him. As he was fortunate, I rejoice at it. As he was valiant, I honour him. But, as he was ambitious, I slew him. There is tears for his love, joy for his fortune, honour for his valour, and death for his ambition."

Julius Caesar, Act 3, Scene 2

"

The game's afoot.
Follow your spirit,
and upon this charge
Cry 'God for Harry,
England, and Saint George!'

"

Henry V, Act 3 Scene 1

"

Some rise by sin,
and some by virtue fall:
Some run from brakes of ice,
and answer none:
And some condemned for
a fault alone.

"

Measure for Measure, Act 2, Scene 1

CHAPTER

four

A Friend
Indeed

For Shakespeare, friendship could be a
source of comfort and joy, as well as one of
great sorrow and anguish. The Bard had
plenty of wise advice to impart when it came
to choosing and valuing our friends.

"

Friendship is constant in all other things Save in the office and affairs of love.

"

***Much Ado About Nothing*, Act 2, Scene 1**

"

Neither a borrower nor
a lender be;
For loan oft loses both
itself and friend,
And borrowing dulls the
edge of husbandry.

"

Hamlet, Act 1, Scene 3

"

A friend should bear his friend's infirmities...

"

Julius Caesar, Act 4, Scene 3

Shakespeare became a wealthy man in his own lifetime. In 1597, he bought *New Place* in Stratford-upon-Avon, one of the largest properties in the town.

He invested widely in land, owned property in London, and was a shareholder in The Lord Chamberlain's Men (later The King's Men) and a part owner of the Globe theatre.

"

If thou wilt lend this money, lend it not
As to thy friends, for when did
friendship take
A breed for barren metal of his friend?
But lend it rather to thine enemy,
Who, if he break, thou mayst
with better face
Exact the penalty.

"

The Merchant of Venice, Act 1, Scene 3

“

Those friends thou hast, and their
adoption tried,
Grapple them unto thy soul with
hoops of steel;
But do not dull thy palm
with entertainment
Of each new-hatch'd,
unfledg'd comrade.

”

Hamlet, Act 1, Scene 3

> **"**
> I would not wish
> Any companion in the
> world but you,
> Nor can imagination
> form a shape
> Besides yourself to like of.

***The Tempest*, Act 3, Scene 1**

Blow, blow, thou winter wind,
Thou art not so unkind
As man's ingratitude;
Thy tooth is not so keen,
Because thou art not seen,
Although thy breath be rude.
Heigh-ho! sing, heigh-ho! unto
the green holly:
Most friendship is feigning, most
loving mere folly.

As You Like It, Act 2, Scene 7

"

But if the while I think on
thee, dear friend,
All losses are restored
and sorrows end.

Sonnet 30

PLAYS COMPARED

Longest play:
Hamlet

Shortest play:
The Comedy of Errors

Shortest scene:
Antony and Cleopatra, Act 3, Scene 9

Bloodiest play:
Titus Andronicus

Most performed play (today):
A Midsummer Night's Dream

Greatest play (arguably):
Hamlet

"

Love, friendship, charity, are subjects all To envious and calumniating time.

"

***Troilus and Cressida*, Act 3, Scene 3**

"

Nature teaches beasts to know their friends.

"

Coriolanus, Act 2, Scene 1

"

That which I would discover

The law of friendship bids me to conceal.

"

The Two Gentlemen of Verona, Act 3, Scene 1

Shakespeare's earliest plays are
Henry VI, Parts I, II & III;
The Two Gentlemen of Verona; and
Titus Andronicus.

The sonnets were also written
around this time, although they
weren't published until 1609.

The Bard's final play is most likely
The Two Noble Kinsmen, which he
co-wrote with John Fletcher in
around 1613.

"

I count myself in nothing else so happy
As in a soul remembering
my good friends;
And, as my fortune ripens
with thy love,
It shall be still thy
true love's recompense.

"

Richard II, Act 2, Scene 3

"

Ceremony was but devised at first
To set a gloss on faint deeds,
hollow welcomes,
Recanting goodness,
sorry ere 'tis shown;
But where there is true friendship,
there needs none.

"

Timon of Athens, Act 1, Scene 2

CHAPTER

five

A Pox Damn You!

When it came to casting a vicious jibe or hurling a stinging barb, Shakespeare was in a league of his own. Indeed, as you'll see in the following quotes, his insults sang with fantastic metaphors and vivid imagery.

"

Away, you three-inch fool!

"

The Taming of the Shrew, Act 4, Scene 1

"
The most infectious pestilence upon thee!
"

Antony and Cleopatra, Act 2, Scene 5

"

Thou elvish-marked, abortive, rooting hog.

"

Richard III, Act 1, Scene 3

Shakespeare had the royal seal
of approval.

His theatre company was often hired
by Elizabeth 1 and James VI of
Scotland and I of England to give
performances at the
royal court.

Out, you mad-headed ape! A weasel hath not such a deal of spleen As you are tossed with.

Henry IV, Part 1, Act 2, Scene 3

"

Away, thou issue of a mangy dog!

"

Timon of Athens, Act 4, Scene 3

" Thou whoreson zed! thou unnecessary letter! "

King Lear, Act 2, Scene 2

"
A pox damn you,
muddy rascal.
"

Henry IV, Part 2, Act 2, Scene 4

"
You Banbury
cheese!
"

The Merry Wives of Windsor, Act 1, Scene 1

"

Why, thou clay-brained guts,
thou knotty-pated fool,
thou whoreson obscene
greasy tallow catch!

Henry IV, Part 1, Act 2, Scene 4

You are not worth the dust which the rude wind Blows in your face.

King Lear, Act 4, Scene 2

"

Out of my sight! Thou dost infect mine eyes.

"

Richard III, Act 1, Scene 2

"

Thou art a boil,
A plague-sore or embossèd carbuncle
In my corrupted blood.

"

King Lear, Act 2, Scene 2

The bubonic plague cast its terrifying shadow over much of Shakespeare's life. In the year of his birth, a quarter of Stratford's population was killed in an outbreak, and between 1603 and 1613, the Globe theatre was shut for a total of 78 weeks to curb infections.

It is fascinating that Shakespeare never directly represents the plague in his plays, though it is frequently referenced in everyday dialogue such as "A plague upon this howling!" (*The Tempest*).

"

Hence, horrible villain,
or I'll spurn thine eyes
Like balls before me;
I'll unhair thy head,
Thou shalt be whipped with wire,
and stewed in brine,
Smarting in ling'ring pickle!

"

Antony and Cleopatra, Act 2, Scene 5

"

You blocks, you stones, you worse than senseless things...

"

Julius Caesar, Act 1, Scene 1

"
O gull! O dolt! As ignorant as dirt!
"

Othello, Act 5, Scene 2

"

The plague of Greece upon thee, thou mongrel beef-witted lord!

"

Troilus and Cressida, Act 2, Scene 1

"

[That] trunk of humours,
that bolting-hutch of beastliness,
that swollen parcel of dropsies,
that huge bombard of sack,
that stuffed cloakbag of guts,
that roasted Manningtree ox with the
pudding in his belly, that reverend Vice,
that gray iniquity, that father ruffian,
that vanity in years?

Henry IV, Part 1, Act 2, Scene 4

O serpent heart, hid with a flowering face! Did ever dragon keep so fair a cave?

Romeo and Juliet, Act 3, Scene 2

"

I do desire we may be better strangers.

"

As You Like It, Act 3, Scene 2

"

Go, prick thy face,
and over-red thy fear,
Thou lily-liver'd boy.

"

Macbeth, Act 5, Scene 3

"

A most notable coward,
an infinite and
endless liar, an hourly
promise-breaker,
the owner of no one
good quality.

"

***All's Well That Ends Well*, Act 3, Scene 6**

"

Marry, his kisses are
Judas's own children.

"

Measure for Measure, Act 3, Scene 2

"

Away, you scullion, you rampallion, you fustilarian! I'll tickle your catastrophe.

"

Henry IV, Part 2, Act 2, Scene 1

"

Tempt not too much the
hatred of my spirit.
For I am sick when I
look on thee.

"

A Midsummer Night's Dream, Act 2, Scene 1

"

A pox o' your throat, you bawling, blasphemous, incharitable dog!

"

The Tempest, **Act 1, Scene 1**

You common cry of curs!
Whose breath I hate
As reek o' the rotten fens,
whose loves I prize
As the dead carcasses
of unburied men
That do corrupt my air,
— I banish you.

Coriolanus, Act 3, Scene 3

"

Thou snail, thou slug, thou sot.

"

The Comedy of Errors, Act 2, Scene 2

"

Sblood, you starveling,
you elfskin,
you dried neat's tongue,
you bull's pizzle,
you stockfish!

"

Henry IV, Part I, Act 2, Scene 4

CHAPTER

six

Blow, Winds!

Whether using a wild tempest to portray human weakness or simply evoking the beauty and grandeur of the world, Shakespeare had much to say about our connection to the natural world. As the following pages reveal, the Bard was a true poet of nature.

"

Blow, winds, and crack your cheeks!
Rage! blow!
You cataracts and hurricanoes, spout

Till you have drench'd our steeples,
drown'd the cocks!
You sulph'rous and thought-executing fires,

Vaunt-couriers to oak-cleaving
thunderbolts,
Singe my white head!

"

King Lear, Act 3, Scene 2

"

And this our life, exempt from public haunt,
Finds tongues in trees, books in the running brooks,
Sermons in stones, and good in everything.

"

As You Like It, Act 2, Scene 1

"

Doubt thou the stars
are fire,
Doubt that the sun
doth move,
Doubt truth to be a liar,
But never doubt I love.

Hamlet, Act 2, Scene 2

Shakespeare's son, Hamnet, died in 1596 when he was 11 years old. The cause of his death is unrecorded, though it is quite possible he died of the bubonic plague – which killed up to a third of children under the age of 12.

Shakespeare's great tragedy *Hamlet*, written between 1599 and 1601, is one letter away from "Hamnet" – and it is tempting to believe that Shakespeare's grief infused his writing.

The spring, the summer,
The childing autumn,
angry winter change
Their wonted liveries;
and the mazèd world
By their increase, now knows
not which is which.

A *Midsummer Night's Dream*, Act 2, Scene 1

"

Under the greenwood tree

Who loves to lie with me,

And turn his merry note

Unto the sweet bird's throat,

Come hither, come hither, come hither:

Here shall he see

No enemy

But winter and rough weather.

As You Like It, Act 2, Scene 5

"

I know a bank where the wild
thyme blows,
Where oxlips and the nodding
violet grows,
Quite over-canopied with
luscious woodbine,
With sweet musk-roses
and with eglantine.

"

A Midsummer Night's Dream, Act 2, Scene 1

"

When I bestride him, I soar; I am
a hawk; he trots the air. The earth
sings when he touches it. The basest
horn of his hoof is more musical
than the pipe of Hermes.

"

Henry V, Act 3, Scene 7

"

Why, what's the matter
That you have such a
February face,
So full of frost, of storm
and cloudiness?

"

Much Ado About Nothing, Act 5, Scene 4

The original Globe theatre was built in 1599. It flourished until 1613, when it caught fire during a performance of *Henry VIII* and burnt to the ground. A second theatre was built to replace it, though it was shut down in 1642 under the Puritan administration.

The current Globe theatre was constructed in 1997. Modelled on the first Globe, it has a thatched roof, ampitheatre-style seating and a stage open to the sky.

"

Look, the world's comforter,
with weary gait,
His day's hot task hath ended in the west,
The owl, night's herald, shrieks, 'tis very late,
The sheep are gone to fold,
birds to their nest;
And coal-black clouds, that shadow
heaven's light,
Do summon us to part, and bid good night.

"

Venus and Adonis

"

When clouds appear, wise
men put on their cloaks;
When great leaves fall, the
winter is at hand;
When the sun sets, who doth
not look for night?

"

Richard III, **Act 2, Scene 3**

My mistress' eyes are nothing like the sun;
Coral is far more red than her lips' red;
If snow be white, why then her breasts are dun;
If hairs be wires, black wires grow on her head.
I have seen roses damask'd, red and white,
But no such roses see I in her cheeks;
And in some perfumes is there more delight
Than in the breath that from my mistress reeks.

Sonnet 130

"

Where the bee sucks, there suck I:
In a cowslip's bell I lie;
There I couch when owls do cry.
On the bat's back I do fly
After summer merrily.
Merrily, merrily, shall I live now
Under the blossom that hangs on the bough.

The Tempest, **Act 5, Scene 1**

When daffodils begin to peer,
With heigh! the doxy, over the dale,
Why, then comes in the
sweet o' the year;
For the red blood reigns in the
winter's pale.
The white sheet bleaching on the hedge,
With heigh! the sweet birds,
O, how they sing!
Doth set my pugging tooth on edge;
For a quart of ale is a dish for a king.

The Winter's Tale, Act 4, Scene 3

INVENTOR OF WORDS

It's estimated that Shakespeare introduced around 1,600 words to the English language. Here are just some of them:

Bedroom	*A Midsummer Night's Dream*
Critic	*Love's Labour Lost*
Downstairs	*Henry IV, Part 1*
Fashionable	*Troilus and Cressida*
Gossip	*The Comedy of Errors*
Jaded	*Henry VI, Part 2*
Lonely	*Coriolanus*
Rant	*Hamlet*
Undress	*The Taming of the Shrew*
Worthless	*The Two Gentlemen of Verona*

"

Like the lily,
That once was
mistress of the field
and flourish'd,
I'll hang my head
and perish.

"

Henry VIII, **Act 3, Scene 1**

When shall we three
meet again?
In thunder, lightning,
or in rain?

Macbeth, **Act 1, Scene 1**

"

The earth, seems to me a sterile promontory; this most excellent canopy, the air — look you, this brave o'erhanging firmament, this majestical roof fretted with golden fire — why, it appears no other thing to me than a foul and pestilent congregation of vapours.

"

Hamlet, **Act 2, Scene 2**

"

This royal throne of kings, this sceptred isle,
This earth of majesty, this seat of Mars,
This other Eden, demi-paradise,
This fortress built by Nature for herself
Against infection and the hand of war,
This happy breed of men, this little world,
This precious stone set in the silver sea,
Which serves it in the office of a wall,
Or as a moat defensive to a house,
Against the envy of less happier lands,
This blessed plot, this earth, this realm, this England...

"

Richard II, Act 2, Scene 1

"

How like a Winter hath
my absence been
From thee, the pleasure of the
fleeting year!
What freezings have I felt,
what dark days seen!
What old December
bareness everywhere!

"

Sonnet 97

There is evidence that Shakespeare wrote a play called *The History of Cardenio* based on a character in Miguel de Cervantes' novel *Don Quixote*. It was performed by The King's Men in 1613, but no manuscript survives.

Love's Labour Won is another Shakespeare play that has possibly been lost to history – although some experts argue that it is an alternative title for *Much Ado About Nothing*.

CHAPTER

seven

To Be or Not to Be...

Shakespeare was a wise observer when it came to understanding the human condition. Love, hate, jealousy, pride, bitterness, life and death – the Bard wasn't short of witty insights, deep reflections and sage advice to share with us.

"

We are such stuff as
dreams are made on,
and our little life is
rounded with a sleep.

"

The Tempest, Act 4, Scene 1

"
Lord, we know what we are, but know not what we may be.
"

Hamlet, Act 4, Scene 5

"

The world is grown so bad That wrens make prey where eagles dare not perch.

"

Richard III, Act 1, Scene 3

"

O, beware, my lord,
of jealousy!
It is the green-eyed
monster which doth mock
The meat it feeds on.

"

Othello, Act 3, Scene 3

> To be, or not to be? That is the question —
> Whether 'tis nobler in the mind to suffer
> The slings and arrows of outrageous fortune,
> Or to take arms against a sea of troubles,
> And, by opposing, end them? To die, to sleep —

Hamlet, Act 3, Scene 1

"

When sorrows come, they come not single spies But in battalions.

"

Hamlet, Act 4, Scene 5

Life's but a walking shadow,
a poor player
That struts and frets his hour
upon the stage,
And then is heard no more. It is a tale
Told by an idiot, full of sound and fury,
Signifying nothing.

Macbeth, Act 5, Scene 5

The man that hath no music in himself,
Nor is not moved with concord of sweet sounds,
Is fit for treasons, stratagems, and spoils.
The motions of his spirit are dull as night,
And his affections dark as Erebus.
Let no such man be trusted. Mark the music.

The Merchant of Venice, **Act 5, Scene 1**

FABULOUS PHRASES

The Bard coined many sayings that have become part of our everyday speech – in fact, it's quite possible you're quoting Shakespeare without even realizing it!

"As good luck would have it"
The Merry Wives of Windsor

"Break the ice"
The Taming of the Shrew

"Cold comfort"
King John

"Devil incarnate"
Titus Andronicus

"What's done is done"
Macbeth

"Wild-goose chase"
Romeo and Juliet

"Too much of a good thing"
As You Like It

"Pound of flesh"
The Merchant of Venice

"It's Greek to me"
Julius Caesar

"Cruel to be kind"
Hamlet

But oh, how bitter
a thing it is to look into
happiness through
another man's eyes.

As You Like It, Act 5, Scene 2

"

All the world's a stage,
And all the men and women
merely players;
They have their exits and
their entrances,
And one man in his time plays
many parts.
His acts being seven ages.

As You Like It, Act 2, Scene 7

Our doubts are traitors,
And make us lose the good we
oft might win
By fearing to attempt.

Measure for Measure, Act 1, Scene 4

All that glisters is not gold —
Often have you heard that told.
Many a man his life hath sold
But my outside to behold.
Gilded tombs do worms enfold.

The Merchant of Venice, Act 2, Scene 7

"

What a piece of work is a man!
How noble in reason, how infinite
in faculty! In form and moving how
express and admirable! In action
how like an angel, in apprehension
how like a god! The beauty of the
world. The paragon of animals.

Hamlet, **Act 2, Scene 2**

"

The web of our life is of a mingled yarn, good and ill together.

"

All's Well That Ends Well, Act 4, Scene 3

"

The robbed that smiles, steals something from the thief.

"

Othello, Act I, Scene 3

"
There is nothing either good or bad, but thinking makes it so.
"

Hamlet, Act 2, Scene 2

"

Brevity is the soul of wit.

"

Hamlet, **Act 2, Scene 2**

As flies to wanton
boys are we to the gods;
They kill us for
their sport.

King Lear, Act 4, Scene 1

"

Love all, trust a few, do wrong to none.

"

All's Well That Ends Well, Act 1, Scene 1

Shakespeare retired to Stratford in 1611, at the age of 47. He looked after his business interests, continued to collaborate with other playwrights and spent time with his family.

It's not known what caused his death, at the age of 52. The date was not recorded, but since we know he was buried on 25 April 1616, and it was customary for burial to occur two days after death, it's quite possible that he died on his birthday, 23 April.

"

how sharper than a serpent's tooth it is To have a thankless child!

"

King Lear, Act 1, Scene 4

"

If everyone knows us and we know none, 'Tis time, I think, to trudge, pack and be gone.

"

The Comedy of Errors, Act 3 Scene 2

"

Better three hours too soon than a minute too late.

"

The Merry Wives of Windsor, Act 2, Scene 2

O, it is excellent
To have a giant's
strength; but it
is tyrannous
To use it like a giant.

Measure for Measure, Act 2, Scene 2

O carve not with thy hours my love's fair brow,

Nor draw no lines there with thine ántique pen.

Him in thy course untainted do allow

For beauty's pattern to succeeding men.

Yet do thy worst, old Time; despite thy wrong,

My love shall in my verse ever live young.

Sonnet 19

"

Have more than thou showest,
Speak less than thou knowest,
Lend less than thou owest,
Ride more than thou goest,
Learn more than thou trowest,
Set less than thou throwest.

"

King Lear, Act 4, Scene 1

Of all base passions,
fear is the most accursed.

King Henry VI, Part 1, Act 5, Scene 2

Shakespeare's gravestone – in Stratford-upon-Avon's Holy Trinity Church – bears the following curse.

"Good friend for Jesus sake forbeare,
To digg the dust encloased heare,
Blest be the man that spares these stones,
And curst be he that moves my bones."

The Bard penned the lines himself, but it appears grave robbers did not pay heed. In 2016, researchers scanned the grave and found the skull was missing.

"

Give every man thine ear,
but few thy voice;
Take each man's censure,
but reserve thy judgement.
Costly thy habit as thy purse can buy,
But not express'd in fancy; rich, not
gaudy;
For the apparel oft proclaims the man...

Hamlet, Act 1, Scene 3

"

Cordelia: Nothing.

Lear: Nothing can come of nothing, speak again.

"

King Lear, Act 1, Scene 1

"

Lord, what fools these mortals be!

"

A Midsummer Night's Dream, Act 3, Scene 2